TOP TWELVE TIPS

for Product Development and Sales

-

Compiled from

The COMPLETE BOOK

of Product Design, Development,

Manufacturing and Sales

Steven Selikoff

Copyright © 2022, 2025

Product Development Academy

ISBN: 9798424383533

To my brother Richard,

You taught me to be an entrepreneur.

You guided me, you believed in me,

you supported me, you listened to me,

you inspired me, and you loved me..

You changed my life, and you made me who I am.

I will miss you forever.

1957 - 2025

Contents

INTRODUCTION 1
#1 THE POWER OF UNIQUE PRODUCTS 3
#2 CUSTOMERS KNOW BEST 7
#3 PROFITABILITY IS KING 15
#4 PRODUCT DESIGN TIPS 19
#5 SOURCING A FACTORY 21
#6 ACT LIKE A SERIOUS BUSINESS 29
#7 NEGOTIATION TIPS 33
    Bonus: Negotiating as a Woman In China 36
#8 HAVE QUALITY INSPECTIONS 37
#9 LOGISTICS 41
#10 RETAIL-READY PACKAGE DESIGN 49
#11 SELLING TO RETAILERS 53
#12 AMAZON AND RETAILERS COMPARED 61
SUMMARY 67

Product-Market Fit
|
customer demand
|
WTP — cost
|
marketing
|
New Product
|
design —— (validate)
|
manufacturing
|
packaging
|
supply chain

Sales **PROFITS**

TOP TWELVE TIPS
For Product Development and Sales

INTRODUCTION

These twelve tips are compiled from *The COMPLETE BOOK of Product Design, Development, Manufacturing and Sales.*

I am a big believer that you should sell your products everywhere customers want to buy. Whether a customer shops from their bed at 2:00 AM, or at a mall, or in-person at their favorite neighborhood store – your product should be in front of them and ready to be bought. Both online, and in physical brick-and-mortar stores.

If you are an Amazon FBA seller you might wonder why I encourage the expansion to selling into physical stores. The answer is simple. According to the US Department of Commerce, in 2024, e-commerce sales, (including Amazon, Temu, TikTok, Shein, Shopify, and others,) accounted for only 16% of total retail sales. Why ignore the other 84% of the market? That's money that belongs in your pocket.

Have you heard gurus say to avoid retail stores? That's because FBA copycat products, even successful ones, sometimes struggle when they are sold from retailer's shelves. We will discuss the reasons for that later within this book. The bigger question is, do products that are successful in stores struggle online? Products that are created with the intent to sell in-store will almost always have great success. On all platforms online, as well as stores. And the combination increases your income dramatically.

Plus, being online and in stores helps sales in both channels. The visibility that comes from selling in stores increases your brand awareness without increasing your marketing costs.

My mother was a teacher. She loved teaching and passed that down to me. I've tried to channel her as I wrote this. If you feel that the way I write sounds like a teacher talking, I take that as a great compliment. She taught me that complex information and new concepts are learned more easily when broken into smaller digestible chunks. With her in mind, I've presented the information in this book within a series of twelve, digestible, 'Top Tips." Within the tips you'll find actionable information about designing products, validation, ensuring profitability, manufacturing, and bringing products to market. There is also a short bonus section about negotiating as a woman in China. That would have pleased her.

Your goal should be to make money. I'd like to help you do that.

- - - - - - - -

If the business model I present here interests you, or you want to learn more, please consider buying the full book - *The COMPLETE BOOK of Product Design, Development, Manufacturing and Sales* - available on Amazon.com

If you want to contact me directly, my email is at the end of this book.

NEVER lose money on a product *"just to learn"* or because you are impatient. Only launch products with the goal of making MONEY.

#1 THE POWER OF UNIQUE PRODUCTS

I am always dismayed when I hear product entrepreneurs boast publicly that their sales are large but confess privately that their profits are small. It happens more often than most people want to admit.

A few years ago, a Redditor posted that he was making more than $6 million dollars a year online but ended with only $47,000 in his pocket. He said he had great reviews and high ranking but had to quit selling because he had to support his family. More than a hundred people responded by saying they had similar experiences.

They are not alone. I was having dinner with an accountant friend of mine who shared a heartbreaking story about an Amazon seller who doubled his sales through incredibly skillful PPC strategy and drove himself to the brink of bankruptcy. I was confused, so he explained to me that doubling the amount of sales when each sale barely broke even, had effectively doubled his inventory and shipping expenses without increasing income. That seller was asked to speak at an Amazon conference and declined because he could not afford the plane ticket and hotel.

Amazon offers incredible opportunities and can provide a great income. Thousands of online Amazon sellers are making a good living, selling profitable products, supporting their families, and putting money in the bank. Yet thousands of others are struggling to pay their monthly bills What's the difference? The successful ones are focused on making money, not just sales.

How do you make money? One of the most critical drivers for a successful brand to be profitable and make money is to start with a product that is unique or significantly differentiated. This is even more important when selling in stores.

Does this mean you need to invent something new and never-before-seen? No, the product merely needs to be innovative enough to be perceived by customers as unique. If a product is successfully differentiated the customer will consider it in a completely different category than it originally was. At that point, in the eyes of the customer, the product has virtually erased its competition.

The accountant friend of mine I mentioned earlier also told me stories of multiple successful Amazon sellers. Every single one of the successful sellers he talked about had differentiated their products in a way that set them apart from the competition. They were not selling copycats, and they were making a lot of money.

Marketing legend Seth Godin uses the metaphor of a purple cow. If you were driving past a field of brown cows, they would all blend together - until you saw a purple cow. That purple cow would grab your attention because among the brown cows, it's unique. What Seth Godin referred to as 'remarkable.'

I experienced this firsthand. My product was simple. Nothing groundbreaking. I sold pillowcases. Just... pillowcases. I didn't invent anything.

Everyone knows what pillowcases are. You've used them your entire life. However, my pillowcases were remarkable because they had cute sayings on them for people who let the dog sleep on the human bed. At that time, 52% of US dog owners let their dog sleep on the bed. For small dogs, the number was much larger, 72%. Yet there was nothing designed specifically for those dog owners. In a world of plain pillowcases, my Dog Snorz pillowcases were unique. Like a purple cow.

Typically, you would not find pillowcases in a pet store. But as a purple cow, Dog Snorz broke that mold. We were sold in hundreds of pet stores and did quite well. This was in addition to home décor, mass market, and linens stores. Customers considered us as a hybrid – both a pet product and pillowcase product. We were in a swamped category, but in their eyes we were different.

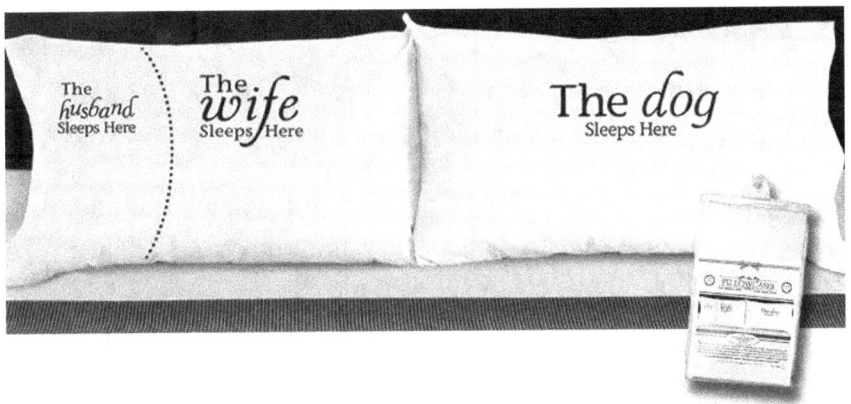

This brings many benefits.

- Unique products stand out and are memorable.
- Unique products are talked about. (Which decreases the cost of marketing.)
- Unique products don't get caught in price wars.
- Unique products give you more control over sourcing costs.
- Unique products are more attractive to retailers and customers.
- Unique products allow you more control over the sales price.
- Unique products can be sold across multiple retail channels. Both online and in stores.
- Unique products enable you to focus on improving your product and scaling, rather than trying to keep up with

competitors. An old boss of mine at Microsoft used to say, "You are either leading or following, and it's always best to lead."

Unique products also come with several challenges.

Upfront costs for unique products may be higher than copycat products. You may need to pay for designers, prototypes, molds, and more. You may have higher initial marketing costs and launch costs. There may also be difficulty in educating consumers about your product and there's the difficulty of not having keywords already associated with your product.

It is important to consider these challenges, and to address these challenges - but don't be afraid of them.

However, there is one risk you need to be frightened of and must take very seriously. What if customers don't buy your product? To succeed you must have customer demand.

A differentiated product with strong customer demand is said to have a good 'Product-Market Fit.'

The best way to ensure product-market fit is to:

    1)   Validate customer demand.
    2)   Use WTP pricing.

WTP stands for Willingness-To-Pay. It's an economic term that describes the price that customers inherently feel is a fair price for your product.

We will discuss validating customer demand, and determining the WTP price, more deeply in the next chapters.

#2 CUSTOMERS KNOW BEST

No matter how important differentiation is, your product should never be different without being something customers want to buy.

Therefore, the primary task you must do BEFORE you start developing a product is to 1) validate customer demand, and 2) fully understand what they would pay for your product.

It's not enough to ask your spouse, your kids or your parents. They love you and they will love your product. That is fantastic for your confidence but is not enough to confirm if you should spend time, spend money, and move forward.

The only way to do that is to find customers (preferably strangers) in your target market and ask them about your product.

Research tools are not enough. There are many data tools and industry surveys that can provide important information about market size, keyword prominence, and the competitive landscape. Amazon FBA sellers may be familiar with tools such as Jungle Scout and Helium 10. When you have a unique or significantly differentiated product the tools and data can provide useful information about your niche or category, but the tools cannot tell you the two most important things you must know.

You must talk to customers to confirm:

- Do customers have a desire or need for YOUR product.
- What is the WTP price for YOUR product.

TOP TWELVE TIPS
For Product Development and Sales

STEP 1 - CONFIRM CUSTOMER DESIRE OR NEED

Someone once said that a product must always solve a problem. They were wrong. A product may also simply fulfill a desire. Or a product can do both, solve a problem and fulfill a desire as well.

For example, a polar fleece hoodie has good insulating properties and keeps you warm. It solves a problem.

A jersey from your favorite sports team fulfills a desire.

A warm hoodie that also has the logo and name of your favorite sports team accomplishes both.

Does that mean a hoodie with a team logo is a winning product? Maybe, but you must still confirm that customers want it.

The USPTO has over 4,400 patents for better mousetraps. Yet there are only a half-dozen or so types of mousetraps that are actually being sold in stores. In fact, the bestselling mousetrap is the very first, and unique snap-trap patented by John Mast in 1903.

Do the other thousands of traps solve a problem? Yes! Yet most customers have no desire to buy them. Wouldn't it be nice if the inventors of the other thousands of mouse traps knew that customers didn't want them before they spent tons of money and time. If they validated customer demand upfront they would have known before they started.

How do you validate that people want your product?

First identify your target customer. These are the people who suffer from the problem your product solves or have a need or desire that your product fulfills.

You need to communicate with them, so figure out how to contact them. Do they attend the same sporting events? Do they shop in the same stores? Do they belong to the same online groups? Meet them where they meet. Whether it's in a Facebook group, a private business club, a church breakfast, or even a boat show. They are the key to success because they are the people who will eventually choose to pay money for your product. Or not.

Ask them these four questions and write down their answers. Try to get at least fifty respondents. More would be much better. (note: Limit yourself to only these questions. Do not overwhelm them with marketing questions yet. You will skew the results.)

    1) Does *[the problem]* affect you?
    2) Would *[the product]* solve the problem?
    3) Would you buy *[the solution/product]* if you could?
    4) How much would you pay for *[the solution/product?]*

In a moment we will discuss the best way to phrase the last question.

Chart your data and remove responses from anyone who answered the first question by saying that the problem doesn't affect them or apply to them.

The remaining responses are your target market. Count how many agreed that your product would solve the problem. If at least half of the respondents feel that your product would effectively solve their problem, then pat yourself on the back. You may have a viable product.

STEP 2 - DETERMINE WTP PRICE

Having everyone agree that a product provides a solution to a problem, and having customers want to buy that product, is not the same thing. Everyone agrees that cars provide transportation, but not everyone agrees on which one they want to buy.

Porsche knew this. When Porsche developed their first SUV, they surveyed customers and sought feedback for every feature. They collected a number of focus groups and asked them about everything. Whenever engineers proposed a new feature, Porsche asked their customers if they wanted it, if they were willing to pay for it, and at times, how much they would pay.

If the customers didn't want it, or wouldn't pay, then the feature was discarded. No matter what.

For example, Porsche asked about cup holders in the SUV. The customers' reaction was an enthusiastic yes. In fact, because they were parents who would carry their kids in the SUV, they asked for more cup holders, and asked for them to be larger. Of course, Porsche complied.

Conversely, when they asked about Porsche's famous six-speed transmission, the customers shocked everyone and said they didn't want it. Porsche listened, and despite the engineers' frustrated complaints and the automotive media's outcry, the six-speed transmission was not included.

What was the result?

The Porsche Cayenne launched to immediate acclaim and became the most successful vehicle in its class, Within ten years, it singlehandedly generated half of Porsche's total profits.

Be like Porsche. ALWAYS confirm that customers not only agree that your product provides a solution (or fulfills a desire) but that customers also say that they will buy it.

Of course that leads to the next obvious question. How much would they pay?

It is critically important to get this right.

When you ask the prospective customer "Would you buy this?" you put them into a purchasing mindset. This creates a bias. If they say yes, they are already imagining themselves making the purchase. That's good. When you follow up with a question about price, they will give you an accurate approximation of what they would imagine paying.

However, there are some people who will never buy your product. No-matter-what. The reason is not important. Their bias towards not needing your product, or not caring about your product, will result in them giving you a price that will be too low.

For example, I do not like asparagus. If you asked me how much I would personally pay for a gourmet asparagus cooker, my answer would always be low because I would never buy one.

Therefore, you need to remove the subjective bias from the question. You can accomplish this by careful phrasing.

Instead of asking, "What would you pay for this?" ask, "If you saw this on the shelf in a store, what do you think the price would be?" The answer you will get is much more unbiased, and objective. And the result will be a much more accurate WTP price.

The WTP price will eventually be the retail price, and this plays perfectly with shopper behavior and psychology.

If you could stand at the end of an aisle and watch new shoppers buy your product you would see the following sequence occur.

First they will stop and pick up your product (assuming you have effective retail-ready packaging.) They will unconsciously form their first opinion based on weight. In most cases, a very light product will feel cheaper compared to a product that is heavier. They will look at the package and try to form an understanding of the product by reading the descriptor on the package, such as Pain Reliever. In effective retail-ready packaging the descriptor is always the first thing that customers read.

Next they will look at the benefits, internalize them and decide if the benefits appeal to them, or solve a problem they have.

At this point, the customer has already formed an expectation of the price they would pay for the benefits they feel they'll receive. That's the WTP price.

Their final step is to look at the price tag on the product, or the price on the shelf. This is the Go / No-Go stage. If the price they see displayed is the same as the WTP price they've already formed in their head then the product goes right into their shopping basket. It's almost instinctive.

If you properly determined your WTP price at the very start of product development, then you will win the shopper every time.

Let's take this a little further. Obviously if the price is too high most people won't buy it. Interestingly it works the other way as well. Prices that are too low create distrust and doubt. They may question the quality, or the amount or size.

If the latest version of an iPhone was on a shelf with a $19.99 price tag people would immediately think it's a toy, a counterfeit, or a fake. They would suspect something was wrong even if it wasn't. The WTP price prevents you from pricing the product too low as well as too high. It gives you the sweet spot every time.

In addition to being the right price for customers, the WTP price is also the right price for retailers. Every time retailers purchase inventory they wonder if the product will sell well, or if it's a dog - that's industry lingo for a product nobody wants. Validating customer demand, and WTP price, prevents retail dogs.

Validation also helps your sales pitch. When you talk to the buyer you will naturally have more confidence. After all you already know that people want it and what they expect to pay.

It doesn't stop there. By basing your manufacturing cost on WTP you are able to sell at the customer preferred price and still make a profit. This increases sales, lowers marketing costs, and makes you more money.

Use WTP as a guide throughout the product design stage as well. Just as Porsche did. Constantly validate customer's WTP price each time you add or remove significant features, decide on the aesthetics, the colors and so on.

Even packaging design should be tested with customers to ensure it reinforces the WTP price.

Validate with customers as much as possible throughout the entire product development process. The customer always knows best …and through validation of demand and the WTP price, you will always know what the customer knows.

That changes everything.

CAUTION!

Eventually you may want to protect your product. If you have shared or published your idea you may risk losing your opportunity for a patent or other protections. Only share general information. **If you must share specific details, always use a confidentiality agreement.**

Download an NDA and always get it signed **BEFORE** discussing any product secrets. This includes customer validation, as well as contests, panels, and masterminds.

#3 PROFITABILITY IS KING

I have been selling products for years, starting in 1973 as a vendor at one of the original Star Trek conventions in New York City, alongside my brother Richard.

I love it, but I would never do this if I were not making money. Neither should you. Your only goal is to make money.

Every veteran of product development will agree on the same thing. You make money on sourcing and manufacturing – not sales. The cost of your product from the factory or supplier must be low enough to make a good profit. If your product cost is not profitable at the very beginning no amount of sales will fix it.

How do you determine projected product cost at the early stages of development? An exact cost is not necessary at this point. You will refine the cost estimate as you progress, but at the start, a close guess is all you need.

Identify an existing product that uses the same materials, that is manufactured the same way, and which is about the same size. Then search for a few versions of that product on Alibaba.com or other sites. Average the listed cost between a few suppliers and the result will be a rough estimate of projected product cost.

Once you have the cost, you have the tools to determine your multiplier. The multiplier is important because a higher multiplier equals higher profits.

Divide the WTP price by the rough product cost. The result is the multiplier. It is usually written as a number followed by an X.

Your goal is to have a 10X multiplier. At a minimum, you should have a 7X multiplier.

If you start with a goal of 10X and a safety net of not going below 7X, you should be profitable even if the product costs fluctuate.

Here's the math.

Imagine that your product is a large stuffed animal with a WTP price of $19.99. The product cost is $2.14/unit for 500 units. Divide $19.99 by $2.14. Your result is the multiplier. In this case it is 9.3X.

Is a 9.3X multiplier possible? Yes!

Sadly, many Amazon FBA coaches and gurus would disagree and claim that regularly achieving high multipliers is impossible. They are wrong and I can prove it.

This example I just gave was not fictional. This example of the stuffed animal occurred as part of my negotiation training at the Canton Fair. You can watch it on YouTube. The video is titled: *Negotiate a 9X Multiplier at the Canton Fair.*
https://youtube.com/shorts/YBkQL-fNzLI

Once you know how to get low product costs you'll be able to do it again and again. This is important. Since you have no direct control over WTP, keeping the product cost low is the best way to attain a high multiplier.

It takes time, skill, and the ability to make quick judgment calls and tradeoffs. Big businesses don't do it this way. In fact, they can't. Instead, large corporations use accountants to set the projected retail price of a product. They take the cost of manufacturing, add other costs and corporate overhead, analyze competitive landscape, and finally come up with the highest retail price 'that the market will bear.'

If the price is higher than customers want to pay they'll spend additional money on marketing and advertising trying to convince customers that the new product is worth more than the customer first expected. Effectively pouring money into raising customer WTP.

This happens more times than you think. I have been part of it a few times in my corporate life, and before that as a photographer in New York City working on major advertising campaigns. I still cringe when I hear corporate managers discuss raising prices as high as the market will bear. I hate that phrase.

You won't use that phrase because you know better. You are different, you're small, you're lean, and you take a smarter approach.

You already know the price of your product on the shelf will be the WTP price. Set by real customers. Not some accountant's fever dream about factories. Unlike large corporations, you won't let manufacturing drive the retail price, you will let the retail price drive the cost of manufacturing.

I am going to repeat this because it is the most important concept in the book, and of WTP product development.

LET THE RETAIL PRICE DRIVE THE COST OF MANUFACTURING.

Calculate your target manufacturing cost and stick to it. The formula is simple. Divide your WTP price by your preferred multiplier. The result is your target product cost. This is the highest you should pay for your product.

Ensure the choices you make during design and manufacturing do not cause your manufacturing costs to exceed your target.

TOP TWELVE TIPS
For Product Development and Sales

- ✓ Make smart decisions during the design stage to stay within your target manufacturing costs.

- ✓ Negotiate with your factory during the manufacturing stage to make sure your target costs are met.

- ✓ Put products on the shelf that people want, at a price they want to pay.

Stay within your target cost and you'll have a high multiplier. A high multiplier turns into a high margin. A high margin results in profits. And high profits means money in your pocket.

Welcome to the beauty of WTP product development.

#4 PRODUCT DESIGN TIPS

Remember the story about the Porsche Cayenne getting feedback from customers? That technique is the foundation of everything I teach, and it's another place where entrepreneurs and small businesses have an advantage over large corporations. You can respond quickly to customer feedback. Large corporations have a lot of processes and politics and committees to go through every time they make a change.

Be self-aware as you go through the design stage. There are a couple of traps that can take you off the track of staying to your target manufacturing cost.

- Scope creep and shiny object syndrome
- Product impatience

The easiest mistake you can make during the design stage is to fall victim to scope creep. Scope creep is adding features to your product that are far from the original vision and increase the scope and cost of your product. A good deterrent to scope creep is to adhere to a well written PRD (Products Requirements Document.) You can find examples of a PRD online and in my book.

Just because somebody's suggestion sounds exciting does not mean it should be included. Stick to your PRD. Do you easily fall victim to shiny-object syndrome? Stick to your PRD.

Steve Jobs was a master at avoiding scope creep. He had a clear vision and never swayed no matter how hard his colleagues and board members wanted to change Apple. He wanted his customers to have the best experience possible, and he avoided shiny object syndrome probably better than any other icon of our time.

Another trap to avoid is product impatience. Many product entrepreneurs are encouraged to jump directly from initial concept to building a prototype. Don't.

Be patient.

Prototypes are useful, but when you first design your product all you need is a sketch. Draw it out. The discipline of sketching your product will force you to analyze each aspect in detail. Often you'll discover where changes need to be made while you sketch. You can also use the sketches to gather customer feedback.

Then, before paying for an expensive high-fidelity prototype, begin with just a rough prototype. You don't need anything fancy. You can use supplies from Home Depot, your own workshop, or craft stores. You are simply looking for proof of concept. Study it. Improve it. And get customer feedback.

Finally, after you have your product mostly figured out you can go build a high-fidelity prototype. You may need a 3D print and a CAD design, which means you may need a product designer or engineer. You can find many of them online or on sites such as Upwork or CADcrowd.com.

This is not a place to skimp on money. Your designer can add to your product to make it more functional, add quality, and make it more appealing. They can help with materials advice and advise ways to keep the costs down.

When your design is done, your job is not over. Once again, go back to your potential customers and 1) validate customer desire or need, and 2) confirm the WTP price has not changed.

#5 SOURCING A FACTORY

Everyone has their own favorite method of finding a supplier. My personal preference is to attend the Canton Fair in China. However, the techniques and information here apply to most other countries as well, including India, Vietnam, Turkey, Cambodia, and the USA.

Is it a Factory or Trading Company

Your primary choice for a supplier is a 'contract manufacturer' (often just called a factory), rather than a reseller or trading company. You will want to have legal agreements between you and the factory, and it is difficult to enforce a binding agreement with an upstream factory if the agreement was only signed by the downstream trading company. Also, as you grow, certain big box retailers may want to audit your factory, and of course you will want to have inspections and your own audits. All of these are difficult, and often impossible if you use a trading company.

Samples

Many Amazon courses teach sellers to ask multiple factories for samples, which they interpret as creating a one-off model of their differentiated design. Then they are instructed to choose the best sample, which they call a 'Golden Sample,' and choose to work with the factory that created it.

I advise differently.

Don't evaluate potential factories by comparing one-off

samples. Use production samples to compare potential factories' standards of production, abilities and quality.

Request samples of existing products taken from actual production runs. These can be overruns of similar products.

Doing this allows you to judge the quality of a typical production run. Products that have passed through an entire assembly line, have been assembled by in-house workers, and have been reviewed by their in-house quality control - which tells you what they consider as acceptable standards. Reviewing samples of actual products that come through their own production line always gives you a much clearer picture of the factory capabilities than a one-off model or sample.

A one-off sample is still valuable, but not before you evaluate all potential factories. Later, after you choose your factory, you can ask for a one-off sample to confirm they understand your specific needs, design, and instructions. This is always a smart step.

Audits

It's best to visit a factory in person. If you cannot do that, having a third-party audit is a good option.

First, it confirms whether the factory is a factory, or if it is a dishonest trading company trying to bluff you. Second, in addition to photographs and videos, it provides you an objective evaluation and review of the factory and gives insight into their strengths, and their weaknesses. Thirdly, not many 'side-gig sellers' do audits. Therefore, it sets you apart from your competition, establishes you as a serious player and helps make the factory take you seriously during negotiations which helps lower prices.

TOP TWELVE TIPS
For Product Development and Sales

Decoy Sourcing

There is a risk that if you disclose your unique product to ten potential suppliers, and choose only one, then the other nine may decide to make your product on their own.

To prevent this, years ago, I formulated a sourcing method called Decoy Sourcing which allows you to compare factories and bids on an 'apples to apples' basis without giving away your secrets. This technique has gained popularity so you may have heard of it already.

Begin by identifying the basic requirements of your product, then apply the same requirements to a fictional product. Choose a decoy, like a toy, that does not let the factory know the real product that you are protecting.

Make sure your decoy has:

- Same general size.
- Same 'look and feel' as your product.
- Same materials requirements.
- Same colors.
- Same printing style (example screen printing.)
- Same technical requirements.
- Same components.
- Same challenges that your product may have.

The decoy does not need to be viable or profitable. It's not important if the factory thinks your product is foolish. It's fictional so none of that matters.

For example, if you are sourcing factories to manufacture a Bluetooth speaker shaped like a leatherbound antique book, you could create a decoy Bluetooth speaker that looks like a small leatherbound gift box.

The gift box should be the same general size and shape of the book. The unique aspect – looking like a book – is different, but the components, materials and design are the same or very similar.

Whichever factory gives you the most confidence that they can produce a gift box speaker, will also give you confidence that they can produce an antique book speaker. You will already know their quality by reviewing their samples. And in addition, whichever gave you the best price for the gift box speaker will also give you the best price for the antique book speaker.

Source with a Decoy Product to prevent the risk of giving away IP secrets.

After the chosen factory signs an NNN to protect your IP you can give them the actual designs. This way, you can be confident none of the factories you rejected know your actual product. (We will discuss NNN agreements in Top Tip #6)

Sending Payment

It is frightening to wire transfer money halfway around the world. But bank wire transfers are not your only choice.

You can pay through Alibaba Trade Assurance, an escrow-based payment system available to people making purchases from Alibaba.com registered suppliers.

If you are not using Alibaba, there are other 3rd party financial services that provide safe payment options as well.

The best way to avoid problems and fraud, however, is to have frequent communication and clear documentation with your supplier.

WeChat

Use WeChat to communicate with your factory. WeChat is the most ubiquitous communication platform in China. You can use it for taxis, also as a payment platform, and its video app works fabulously. It does almost everything.

But the most important reason to use WeChat is that it shows your supplier that you understand the Chinese business culture, and you know their preferred platform. Using it sets you apart from the competition. All these little things help build a good impression with your factory and that translates into lower costs and less delays.

There is a very clever sourcing trick you can use if you are communicating via WeChat.

In the middle of one of your video calls, spontaneously ask the sales rep to show you the production floor. If the supplier is a factory, the production floor should be close. Perhaps in the same building, or next door. They will happily say, Yes.

If they are a trading company and have been deceiving you, they will make up an excuse to delay showing the factory for a day or two. This is a red flag. Drop them.

If you are not sure whether you are dealing with a factory or a trading company, use this trick to confirm whether it is one or the other.

Ask to see the factory.
Factories invest a lot in equipment and machinery. A trading company will not have a production floor and expensive machinery.

#6 ACT LIKE A SERIOUS BUSINESS

If your product and brand takes off, and I hope it does, you may wake up one day to a million-dollar purchase order. Or more.

It's not impossible. So be prepared. Manage your business professionally from the very beginning.

Start by setting up your company as a corporate entity. That could be a LLC, a Corp, a PTY, a LTD, and so on.

Place your bank accounts, your agreements, and your IP all under your corporate entity. This way you won't comingle your assets. When you exit (sell your company) you will be able to hand over a neatly wrapped package. This builds confidence in the buyer and can dramatically increase the amount they'll pay.

Hire a local accountant that you can meet with in person. Educate yourself about business accounting and learn about financial reports.

Have your accountant regularly review your revenue, expenses and profits. Have them prepare your Balance Sheet, P&L Statement, and Cash Flow Analysis. If you are unfamiliar with any of these, ask your accountant to teach you about them. It is imperative that you understand your finances.

In addition to an accountant, you should have a business attorney, plus, have an IP attorney. An IP attorney is not the same as a typical business attorney. They specialize in intellectual property protection. They have additional training and pass an additional bar exam to be certified.

Work with your IP attorney to build a strategy for protecting and defending your intellectual property. This may include trademarks, patents, copyrights, and other tools such as recordation. They will also be your first resource if you discover someone infringing on your intellectual property. You are in the big leagues now, so be prepared to seek redress and resolve issues through the courts, not Amazon. You will be thankful for it later.

- ✓ Pro Tip 1: Some gurus recommend filing a class 35 trademark as an umbrella to cover any future products while paying for only a single class. Don't do it. It won't hold up in court, and it might be treated as fraud.

- ✓ Pro Tip 2: Once you have your trademark, record it with Customs and Border Protection. It costs around $190 for ten years. Anyone besides you that tries to import your trademarked goods will have them confiscated at the border.

- ✓ Pro Tip 3: Some people think you can circumvent patent protection on a product if you change 25%. This is a myth, and frankly it doesn't make sense. If you think you might be infringing on someone's patent, always consult an attorney.

You should also protect yourself through proper documentation, contracts, and agreements. Use an NDA when appropriate and understand its limitations. Make sure that your significant business purchases, from molds to inventory to certifications clearly state your ownership or involvement. Make sure your business operating agreements and equity agreements are properly structured and signed. An email between folks promising equity in a company without a signed agreement, and without proper structure, is an invitation for conflict and misinterpretation.

In China, protect yourself with an NNN. That is a Non-Disclose, Non-Use, Non-Circumvent agreement. This is a contractual agreement which prevents the supplier from telling others about your product, selling your product, and offering your product to your retailers or online. You can download an NNN from my website, ProductDevelopmentAcademy.com under the 'Downloads' tab.

Finally, as a business, make sure you have addressed responsibilities such as insurance, taxes, filings, and financing. Don't ignore these.

TOP TWELVE TIPS
For Product Development and Sales

Visit your factory. Learn how your product is made. Research. The more you know about manufacturing your product the better you will be able to negotiate.

#7 NEGOTIATION TIPS

The goal of negotiation is more than a good price; it's a good relationship. In China this is *Guanxi*. Don't approach negotiation with a transactional mindset, like buying a car. Seek a long-term, mutually beneficial relationship.

Unfortunately, there are way too many subtleties and techniques involved in successful negotiation to cover everything in this condensed overview book. Therefore, in this chapter I will simply cover six of the most useful tips.

1) Before you begin negotiating you should prepare yourself by studying and understanding the manufacturing process and the materials used in your product. There are a lot of videos on YouTube that will teach you how things are made. You can easily learn about jacquard knits, plastic injection, glass casting, PCBs, and warp versus weft threads by watching videos. Do your research upfront, so that when you start talking with a supplier, you are already familiar with the processes, labor, materials, and other factors that go into your product.

2) Be patient. When I teach people about negotiation with Chinese suppliers, I call it "the Long Dance," a term I started years ago but is as applicable today as it was back then.

   Never rush your negotiation. Take your time. Do not appear desperate. You aren't desperate, so don't let your nerves make that impression.

If you are in China when you negotiate, expect at least a day-long affair.

They will show you the factory and perhaps make a fancy presentation about themselves and their history. This is a great way to learn about them, and to learn what principles guide their business. They will offer food and make small talk. They may even make tea for you in an elaborate ceremony.

Their goal is to learn about you. They want to understand your business. Sincere factories do this to build a relationship. But factories will also use these conversations to form opinions about you, your business experience, and your integrity. Allow them to see that you are decisive, humble, and professional. Always show respect and courtesy.

A large lunch will probably be offered, which they will pay for. Be respectful and gracious for their outlay. Do not discuss product price during lunch.

Afterwards you will return to the factory. They may show you more samples. Be patient. Discussion of price may seem to never come. When it does, negotiate professionally. Once negotiations are concluded you may be offered dinner or drinks. Do not get drunk. It will not lead to anything positive.

3) You should also be patient and expect the long dance when you negotiate remotely. Do not expect to ask for a price, get an answer, and be done with business in 5 minutes time. Conversely, do not accept the first price that they offer. After they offer a price, tell them about your product and your business plan. Then present your counteroffer.

4) Only accept a price if it is the RIGHT price. What is the right

price? This is the target manufacturing cost you figured out earlier. Start low and slowly build up to your target manufacturing cost.

5) In China, Kings negotiate with Kings. YOU are the owner or founder of your business. Do not pretend to be a middle manager or procurement manager. Don't cry and say that your boss will fire you if they don't give you a price.

It's pathetic and your supplier's sales agent knows it is a lie. They watch YouTube too. Eventually you will have to confess the truth, which is extremely awkward.

Furthermore, you have demonstrated to them that you are inexperienced, dishonest, and insecure. That's not how you want to be seen.

6) Never forget to discuss MOQ and payment terms. Do you want to pay 30 days after receipt? 60 days? Do you want to place a low deposit? Now is the time to discuss these aspects of your purchase. EVERYTHING is negotiable.

A successful negotiation ends with both sides in partnership.

Bonus: Negotiating as a Woman In China

Chinese culture has built-in sexism and treats women, unfairly, as secondary to men. It's part of their culture and the same thing is true of many other countries and cultures around the world. You will see this throughout all levels of society and business in China. In China however, there is a fascinating exception.

In the late 1970's and early 80's the central government of China initiated a controversial One-Child policy. Its purpose was to reduce the growth rate of China's exploding population. An unintended consequence of this policy was that business owners who had only a female child, raised her to run their business.

Today a lot of those original business owners have retired. Their daughters have stepped into their roles, and are leading large companies like media companies, mining companies, real estate companies, and more. This also applies to factories.

These powerful, intelligent, and respected women have created a third unique social class. Higher than men. They are super-women business leaders.

As a female business owner, you can stand up and put yourself into their super-woman class as well. Even if you are a Westerner.

You'll notice them at the Canton Fair. You'll occasionally see them on Chinese TV. Often they'll wear the unofficial uniform of a simple black blazer. Watch them and emulate their business demeanor. They are unapologetic and they often take strong positions when negotiating.

Use this to your advantage. Put a stoic expression on your face and confidently push back on price. Frequently you will get more concessions from the factory than your male counterparts.

Try it. You will be happily surprised.

#8 HAVE QUALITY INSPECTIONS

Always have a pre-shipment inspection. Every single time!

You may trust your factory, but machinery may break, workers may retire, and new workers may need to be trained. All of these may cause defects. Their internal QA should catch them, but it's your responsibility to double check.

Never have the inspection done by your freight forwarder, nor your sourcing agent, nor your Amazon prep company, nor your supplier. All those companies financially benefit by approving defective merchandise. Only use licensed 3rd party inspection companies. They will be honest and will call out all defects they find.

Ask for an AQL inspection. AQL stands for 'Acceptable Quality Limits', which represents the maximum number of defects tolerable within the standards set by ISO 2859-1. If the defects exceed the AQL level, the entire production run is rejected.

Defects are classified as Minor, Major, and Critical. You may be new to AQL standards, but your Chinese factories are already familiar with them. The inspection agency will select a small percentage of random units to inspect. The number they choose have been statistically proven to show an accurate evaluation of the defect rate of a production run.

Many people ask why they shouldn't do a 100% inspection. It makes sense for a run of 200 products. But if you do 2,000 products a 100% inspection becomes unreasonable and unreliable.

Assume a careful inspection of your products takes 5 minutes each. A 100% inspection of 200 will take about two days. Two inspectors working at the same time could complete it in one day.

A 2,000-unit order would take almost 4 weeks, at 8 hours a day. The time is unreasonable, and you can be sure that the monotony would result in the inspector eventually missing some defects. Plus, the cost would be extremely high.

An inspection randomly sampled to AQL standards will give you the same results in less time and at a lower cost.

Let's look more closely at the three levels of defects.

Critical defects can cause harm or injury or invalidate certifications. Even a single unit with a critical defect will cause the entire production to fail inspection.

Major defects are defects that materially lessen the value of a product such as dents in a cutting board or headlights on an RC car that do not light up.

Minor defects are mostly cosmetic, such as small scratches, slight color variations, loose threads, or minor dents.

A standard Level II inspection allows ZERO Critical defects, 2.5% Major defects, and 4% Minor defects. If the inspector finds that the number of defects equal or exceed these parameters the inspection is failed.

Finally, you should always pay the inspection company, for every inspection performed. Despite what you may see in Facebook groups and on YouTube, never have your supplier pay for the second inspection. You should pay for the second inspection and have the factory reimburse you. The inspection company works for the person who pays them, and that should always be you.

TOP TWELVE TIPS
For Product Development and Sales

TOP TWELVE TIPS
For Product Development and Sales

#9 LOGISTICS

There are three forms of shipping to consider. Air Courier (also known as Air Express,) Air Freight (also known as Air Cargo,) and Ocean Freight.

Air Courier is the fastest and the most expensive. Courier companies include FedEx and DHL. You might save money by using your own account and paying the courier fees yourself. You can also ask your factory to arrange it, which in some cases, may cost less. Frankly, I always ask the factory for their cost and compare it to my own account. Frequently the factory gets a better rate.

Air Cargo is sent in containers within the belly of commercial flights. It may take a circuitous route to get to you over a few days or weeks, but it is usually faster than ocean freight. It is also more expensive than ocean freight (but less expensive than courier.)

Ocean Freight means putting your products into a shipping container and then putting that container onto a boat. At both ends of the journey it must pass through a port and Customs.

There are a lot of fees that are attached to ocean freight, such as ISF fees and port fees that do not apply to air cargo. Therefore, for small orders always check the rates of each. Surprisingly, sometimes air cargo costs less than ocean freight for small orders.

Shipping is usually arranged through a Freight Forwarder. You can find freight forwarders online, meet them at the Canton Fair, find them on Alibaba, and simplest of all, your factory can recommend a freight forwarder that they have history with and whom they trust.

Many people ask me how to check out their freight forwarder. The US Federal Maritime Commission publishes a list of freight forwarders that are registered and licensed, and most importantly, whom you can pursue for recourse in the US courts if things go wrong. If your freight forwarder is not on the FMC list then you have very limited opportunities to hold them legally accountable if they do anything shady. Most freight forwarders want to be on the list. Any forwarder from any country can register. Therefore, if your freight forwarder is not on the FMC list there is a good chance they do not want to be held accountable for lies they tell you and fraudulent practices.

When you ship by ocean you will be faced with a choice of shipping methods indicated by three-letter acronyms. These are 'incoterms' which are internationally recognized rules that define who is responsible for shipping, insurance, customs clearance, and duties at different stages of the supply chain.

There are 11 accepted incoterms. Three common incoterms are:

> FOB – Free On Board
>
> EXW – Ex Works
>
> DDP – Delivered Duty Paid

It is very helpful to understand the differences before you choose which method to use. Gurus and YouTube videos advise entrepreneurs to use DDP because it is simplest. However, the lack of transparency, the opportunities for fraud, and the financial risk may make you think otherwise. Let's have a more detailed look at each of these three incoterms.

FOB

The factory delivers the cargo to the port. Ownership and responsibility are transferred to you once the cargo is on board. Once the ship leaves port you will receive a Bill of Lading which documents which container holds your products and which ship they are on. Upon arrival at the US port, you are responsible for paying duties and tariffs. This process applies to 10 of the 11 incoterms. Only DDP does not provide you with a Bill of Lading or any other documentation.

EXW

Your freight forwarder picks up the cargo at the factory. Ownership and responsibility are transferred to you once the cargo leaves the factory. Just like FOB, once the ship leaves port you will receive a Bill of Lading which documents which container holds your products and which ship they are on. Upon arrival at the US port, you are responsible for paying duties and tariffs.

DDP

Your freight forwarder either picks up the products from the factory, or the factory delivers them to the freight forwarder at the port. From this point onward, DDP is very different than any other incoterm.

Here are some examples of how DDP is not the same as other incoterms, and how shady freight forwarders can take advantage of the system.

Who owns your goods?

Ownership of your goods remains with the factory or is transferred to the Freight Forwarder. Not to you. To be clear, you are not the owner, even if you have paid your supplier in full. Your goods will sit in a warehouse until the freight forwarder puts them on a ship of the freight forwarder's choosing. This may be the ship you originally paid for, but commonly it is a different ship. They own the goods, so it is their choice. There is no visibility or official documentation so you will never know.

Is there proof that your goods are on the right ship?

For any other incoterm this would be the Bill of Lading. However, you do not receive a Bill of Lading using DDP because you do not own your goods until ownership is transferred upon final delivery. Therefore, you have no documentation confirming which container and ship your products are on. In fact, you have no visibility to any official documentation at all, which unfortunately allows a lot of abuse of the process.

What if they make a mistake or falsify claims to Customs.

Upon arrival at the US port, the freight forwarder is responsible for paying duties and tariffs. However, you are ultimately still legally accountable if they make an error. If they undercount or undervalue your shipment, eventually you will have to pay the duty plus fines. If it's done intentionally you could also face jail time.

Should you buy insurance?

You cannot get insurance when you ship DDP because you do not own the goods. Despite this, many shady freight forwarders will offer insurance on DDP shipments. This is a scam. Do not buy it. You cannot get insurance on something you do not own. The freight forwarder is taking advantage of you and assumes that you do not know the rules of DDP.

Is DDP the only way to get door-to-door service?

No. Every freight forwarder can arrange domestic transportation. DDP does not mean door-to-door.

Many DDP shipping sales agents in Facebook groups claim that there are no duties or tariffs with DDP. This is not true. Of course, there are duties and tariffs just like any other incoterm. However, they are paid by the freight forwarder.

Unfortunately, shady freight forwarders often undercount the amount of product in the container or undervalues the goods in order to pay less than the required amount. The bad news is that as Importer of Record or Consignee, you are ultimately accountable even if your favorite Facebook freight forwarder was the one that did the illegal acts.

If this is discovered, even years later, Customs and Border Protection, can impose civil penalties including fines, seizure and financial penalties up to two times the amount of the original duties due.

Customs and Border protection can impose criminal penalties if the violation was made with intent, fraud, or is smuggling. Smuggling seems farfetched but shady freight forwarders don't declare goods, leave products off the manifest and off the Entry Summary all the time. If your products are brought into the US without being declared you are technically smuggling.

Punishments include additional fines, and imprisonment up to five years.

It would be nice if you could sue the freight forwarder for all that bad behavior, but if they are not registered with the Federal Maritime Commission then you can't.

How common is DDP fraud?

Whenever I am around a large number of Amazon sellers I ask the following question. "How long does it take to go through US Customs?"

At least 80% of people respond with times ranging from one week to thirty days. None of those are true. Customs takes less than a minute or two and can occur 5 days before reaching port. The process is done online with the submission of a Form 7501, also called an Entry Summary.

Why do shady freight forwarders tell you it takes a long time to go through customs if it really only takes minutes online? They lie about Customs time because they are not shipping your goods on the vessel that you paid for. Your goods are on a cheaper slower vessel. The fables about customs delays are an excuse to hide the difference between the arrival date of the promised vessel and the actual arrival date of the cheaper alternative.

What happens if you have a large order? In that case, a shady freight forwarder will split your goods into two containers on two ships. Or more. And it may take longer.

Sometimes a shady freight forwarder will justify the extended delay by saying that your goods are being examined by customs. In most cases this too is a lie. Customs examines approximately 3% of containers, and of those, most examinations take just a day or two.

In the last 20 years I have heard an amazing number of scams. Some of which are very creative. Some dishonest freight forwarders will charge you for fictional services, or offer you non-existent insurance policies.

DDP is a serious and legitimate method of shipping. The problem is that the lack of transparency and documentation has allowed dishonest practices to thrive. Don't risk your business. The easiest way to tell who can be trusted, and who cannot be trusted, is to always check if they are listed on the FMC list.

The FMC site is: https://www2.fmc.gov/oti

TOP TWELVE TIPS
For Product Development and Sales

64% of in-store Shoppers say they will buy a product right off the shelf, if they like the packaging, WITHOUT any further research.

TOP TWELVE TIPS
For Product Development and Sales

#10 RETAIL-READY PACKAGE DESIGN

One of the most important differences between e-commerce and selling to retailers is packaging. Your product, sitting on a shelf, does not have the benefit of a detailed description, explanation of benefits, multiple photos, explainer videos, nor any of the other tools that a listing provides to communicate and sell to a customer. Your package must do all of that. Plus, it must capture the attention of a shopper and be compelling enough for them to pick it up off the shelf. All of this within a fraction of a second surrounded by other goods competing for attention.

Bad packaging can sink a product. Good packaging can create explosive sales. A mentor of mine once pointed out that when customers are inside the store, they buy the box, not the product.

Be extremely selective when you choose a packaging designer. A recent search on Fiverr listed 8,917 providers offering package design. I would bet that only a few have actual retail package experience or understand the unique needs of retail packaging design. Retail packaging and e-commerce packaging have different goals. Therefore, retail package design is different than e-commerce design.

In 2006, Walgreens invited me to their headquarters to present my weight-loss product. It had been selling very well online and was the darling of influential bloggers. It was even written up in national women's magazines. None of these platforms showed the retail packaging, so when Walgreens invited me they had never seen the package. Even though I hired a professional designer, they were not experienced with the requirements of retail packaging, and when

Walgreens saw my packaging, they rejected my product and dismissed me for being inexperienced.

Your package **must** communicate the following, in this order:

1) What is the Product (descriptive product name)
2) What are the Benefits
3) What are the Features (and USP)

In addition, your product should have shelf impact to draw shopper attention while always communicating its brand. This builds interest, creates confidence, enhances credibility, and results in sales.

Brand should be established graphically and with visual clues, and at the same time illustrate the differences between products within the same product line. These elements are often in a Brand Guide.

- ✓ Pro Tip 1: Your retail package should have a GS1 UPC code on it. The Amazon FNSKU code is not compatible with retail scanning systems.

- ✓ Pro Tip 2: Research the legal labeling and certification requirements for your specific product. Care labels, electronics certifications, safety warnings, law labels, nutrition labels, suffocation warnings, and of course Country of Origin, are all examples of very specific information that must be included on the label or package.

- ✓ Pro Tip 3: Once your package design is complete, put it in front of strangers for their reaction, just like you did with Customer Demand Validation. Do not tell the person what your product is, or why they should buy it. Ask them to look at the package and then describe the product and its benefits to you. If they can do that quickly and correctly, you have a winner. If they can't, go back to the drawing board.

Finally, most e-commerce sellers understand the importance of visuals and the impact of lifestyle photos. The same is true for retail. A good lifestyle image can show a feature but can also convey emotion, and emotion can convey benefits.

A good photo can also add to shelf impact. Your package must stand out on the shelves. Therefore, always consider including great photography when designing your package. (And always validate the package with strangers.)

TOP TWELVE TIPS
For Product Development and Sales

#11 SELLING TO RETAILERS

There are two major categories of brick-and-mortar retailers. The categories are based on number of stores in the chain, the amount of sales, the store size, the processes for pitching, receiving payments, and who the decision maker is.

- Independent and Specialty retailers
- Big Box stores

Independent and Specialty retailers (often called Mom & Pop stores by people not professionally experienced within the industry,) are physically smaller than big box stores, are either a single entity or are part of a small chain, and the owner is often on site.

They have a smaller selection in their stores, and less foot traffic. They have smaller budgets and buy in smaller amounts.

However, they make immediate buying decisions, pay upfront, and pay for shipping. This is a great benefit to small businesses like yours, and the reason many first-time sellers begin with independent and specialty stores.

They personalize the display of your product, (called merchandising,) and they are more open to taking risks on new unproven products. Therefore, independent and specialty retailers are great for launching new products.

Examples of Independent and Specialty retailers are: Gift Shops, Small Chains, Boutiques, Home Décor Stores, Health Stores,

Independent Pet Stores, Kitchen Stores, Garden Centers, Resort Stores, Electronic Stores, Bookstores, Candy Stores, Cigar Stores, Religious Stores, Wedding Stores, Holiday Stores, Furniture Stores, Hallmark Stores, Souvenir Stores, Game Stores, Gym Stores, Hospital Gift Shops, Craft Stores, University Stores, and more.

In comparison, big box retailers are physically larger, typically more than 50,000 sq. feet, and sometimes as much as 200,000 sq. feet.

They are part of a large corporation and buying decisions are handled by a Category Buyer sitting in an office probably located in the corporate headquarters. The buyer has responsibility for placing products in hundreds, and sometimes thousands of stores.

Big box stores often anchor shopping malls and are surrounded by parking lots. The expectation is that shoppers will buy so much that they will fill shopping carts and need cars to drive home..

Their budgets are large, and the purchasing process is much longer than Independent and Specialty stores.

If a buyer wants to sell your product in their stores you will be assigned a Vendor Number and be onboarded. Then you will have an in-store test of 50-200 stores. Based on the results of the test, you may be rolled out to the rest of their chain. This could be hundreds, or even thousands of individual stores.

Examples of Big Box stores are: Walmart, Target, Home Depot, Costco, Lowes, Bunnings, Nordstrom, Michaels, Dollar General, Kohls, Publix, Hudson Bay, PetSmart, CVS, Petco, Dollar Tree, Tesco, Aldi's, Old Navy, Kroger, Walgreens, Office Depot, Albertsons, REI, Woolworth, Sainsbury's, Ross, Cabela's, Fred Meyer, Schnucks, Rite Aid, Ulta Beauty, Sharper Image, Canadian Tire, and more

Independent and Specialty stores keystone the prices on the shelf. This means they charge the customers twice as much as they pay you. This is also called a 50% margin, or a 100% markup.

Big Box stores have specific margins depending on the product and category. However, for business planning purposes, you can use the keystone formula as a generic approximation.

Selling to both big box and independent & specialty retailers can be boiled down to meeting their needs. If your product fits their needs, you are 90% on the way to a sale.

Some of their needs are:

- A product that increases store profits.
- A product that fits their store and customers.
- A product that is new or different.
- A product that adds to the customer market basket.
- A product that does not cannibalize existing products.
- A product with an appealing price.
- A reliable manufacturer with a dependable supply;.
- A product that has good packaging and shelf impact.
- A product that is part of a full brand.
- A product that has a proven history of sales.

This may seem like a daunting list, but as you can see, you already know how to meet some of these criteria.

Validate customer demand, have a unique product, properly vet your factory so you can be confident of a reliable supply, choose a 3PL with retail experience, and have excellent retail-ready packaging. Since you started with WTP pricing you know that the retail price will be the price customers want to pay.

Most importantly, although it is not on the retailer list, is that you have a high multiplier which means you will be making profits, not just sales.

Retailers have to choose which products go onto their shelves very carefully. Every inch on every shelf in a retailer should bring in profit. They do not want one product sitting on a shelf that takes away sales of another existing product. That is known as cannibalizing another.

This is the biggest challenge for Amazon sellers when starting to sell in physical retailers. Retailers lose money if your product takes sales away from an existing product because they have lost potential revenue and shelf space where another product could sit and bring in money.

This is the exact opposite of what Amazon FBA sellers are taught. The FBA method is to use tools such as Helium 10 to identify successful products, copy them, and then take away their market share. That's cannibalization.

Amazon corporate loves cannibalization because Amazon profits whenever Amazon sellers compete for sales, especially when both competitors pay Amazon for advertising. Since Amazon has virtual shelves, not physical ones, they can put as many competitive sellers on the shelf as they want. In fact, the more sellers they have competing with similar products, the more money they make from each of them

This brings us back to the very first topic we discussed. Make your product unique or significantly differentiated. If you are a purple cow among brown cows then customers won't consider you in the same category as your competitors, and you won't have to pay as much advertising. As a bonus, you won't be cannibalizing products on store shelves, so retailers will love you too.

There are lots of ways to meet and connect with retailers. Tradeshows, LinkedIn, Email, and even Google all work well. Connecting with big box stores are a bit harder. You should start with emails which can usually be found online with some hard work. Or you can use online B2B portals such as RangeMe and Faire.

Personally, I prefer face-to-face meetings. Therefore, one of my favorite ways to pitch my products to big box stores is through their open calls.

Open calls are a yearly event held by big box retailers where entrepreneurs and small businesses just like you get to pitch their products directly to category buyers.

LOWE'S - Lowe's hosts the "Into The Blue: Lowe's Product Pitch Event" every March. If you win, you receive a "Golden Ticket" to pitch your products directly to Lowe's buyers.

COSTCO - April is the month for Costco's open-call event, where winners get the chance to present their products to Costco buyers.

TARGET - In May, Target holds the "Target Open House" event. Winners get an opportunity to present their products to Target buyers.

CVS - Also in May, CVS looks for health-related and innovative products during their open call. Winners are invited to pitch their products to CVS buyers.

KROGER - Kroger's open call event occurs in June. Winners receive the chance to pitch their products to Kroger buyers.

WEGMANS - Similarly, Wegmans holds their open call event in June, with winners getting the chance to present to Wegmans buyers.

HOME DEPOT - Home Depot's open call event takes place in August. Winners receive a "Golden Ticket" to pitch their products to Home Depot buyers.

WALMART - Walmart's Open Call event is in September. Winners receive a "Golden Ticket," giving them the opportunity to do business with Walmart. Products must be made, grown, or assembled in the USA.

BEST BUY - Finally, in October, Best Buy holds its open call event. Winners get the chance to present their products to Best Buy buyers.

Every retailer listed here specifically states in their open-call announcements that they want products that are new and innovative. Once again, that takes us back to the 'purple cow' concept we've discussed a few times in this book.

You can find information about open calls on each of the retailers websites.

Add to that the validation of customer demand and WTP pricing and you can be confident you are well on your way to retailer success.

TOP TWELVE TIPS
For Product Development and Sales

Bonus – When To Say No

Not all retailers are the same. Sometimes the best choice you can make is to say No.

You want retailers that pay your invoices. Therefore, you want to avoid retailers that have financial trouble. Years ago, before they went out of business in the US, I was offered an extremely large PO by K-Mart. My financing team told me that they were overextended and had stopped paying some of their invoices. I declined K-Mart's offer. That eventually proved to be a very smart choice.

How do you know if a retailer has financial issues? If you use a factoring company you can ask them. Their business is built on retailers eventually paying their bills, so they always have the latest and best information.

You should also avoid off-price retailers and discount retailers until your product line has reached the end of its life. Off-price retailers such as T.J.Maxx and Ross offer their customers very low prices. But to accomplish that, they will pay you much less than your fair market price.

I am not saying that they are a bad store. But I am saying that you should know that an off-price retailer is not the same as Target or Walmart.

Worse, other retailers will not want to buy your products once they are for sale in an off-price store.

Since they pay you less than your standard price they are also a very easy sale. They rarely say no if you lower your price enough. That means even the most questionable sales rep can always sell to T.J.Maxx and other off-price retailers.

At almost every trade show where I sell products, a questionable looking, fast-talking, sales rep will approach me and promise me great success if I hire them. They all boast about their prowess and promise that they can get me into T.J.Maxx very easily. Obviously I say no.

Shady reps like that are always looking for entrepreneurs with very little experience and try to impress them. They are so common at trade shows that they are joked about by vendors after show hours.

Feel free to say no to off-priced retailers (unless they are part of your deliberate strategy) and say no to retailers that are financially unstable. I've seen too many Amazon sellers lose money because they said yes to the wrong retailer. You've worked too hard on your business to settle for less than you deserve.

#12 AMAZON AND RETAILERS COMPARED

The fundamental principles of selling online and selling in stores are the same. However, there are some differences in the details between the two that may trip you up if you only have experience online.

UPC Code

Retailers require a UPC code, not an Amazon FNSKU. Only buy your UPC code directly from GS1.

In 1973 a consortium of large retail stores wanted to streamline the checkout process. They formed an organization and created the UPC barcode.

That organization was later renamed GS1. At that time some vendors with unlimited barcodes sued for the right to continue selling them. They won the right to sell them, but retailers were not forced to honor them or make the point-of-sale systems recognize them. Retailers will only recognize barcodes purchased directly from GS1. It's no surprise. Since retailers formed GS1, it's easy to understand why retailers want to support GS1 barcodes.

Retail-Ready Packaging

Packaging for online sales, and packaging for physical retailers have different objectives. When you sell online you have a lot of opportunities to communicate to the shopper. When you are on the shelf you only have the facing of the box.

Your package must get the shopper's attention, tell them what the product is, what it does, the benefits of the product, the USP, and reinforce the previously identified WTP price. Or make it higher. All this while giving the shopper confidence and letting them know the brand and value. That's a lot to ask of one clean, easy-to-read, relatively small, box..

Be sure to always follow the retail-ready packaging tips discussed earlier.

Keystone Prices

Retailers keystone prices, which means they charge customers twice as much as the wholesale price they paid you.

Since Amazon now takes about 50% of what customers pay for your product, it should not be much of a change.

Do Not Cannibalize

We discussed cannibalization earlier and by now you should understand the importance and benefits of being significantly differentiated or unique. There is another aspect which we haven't talked about yet. Trade dress violations.

If your product appears so visually similar to an existing product, that a customer may confuse the two, you may be infringing on their trade dress. This could lead to very messy and expensive lawsuits. Big box retailers do not want to have any of the drama or risk of potential lawsuits. Therefore, if they have any concern that your product may possibly be mistaken as another brand's product, they will refuse to carry you.

This is true even if they do not carry the other product.

Do Not Underprice Your Retailers

Retailers do not want you to draw customers away from their stores. If you get a reputation of offering lower prices on Amazon or on your site, than in the store, they will drop you.

OTIF

Amazon sellers may be used to shipments arriving late, or with less product than they ordered. Retailers will not stand for that. When a retailer sets a date and time for your delivery to their warehouse or distribution center they expect you to deliver OTIF. That stands for On-Time, and In-Full. This is so important that big box stores charge large fines for late, or less-than-full deliveries. You may even be dropped.

Stay In Stock

Almost every Amazon seller knows the frustration of running out of stock. Your ranking suffers, you lose potential sales, and you pray every day that your products show up.

When you sell to retailers you can never be out of stock. Make sure you understand your inventory trends and be prepared.

Retailers Buy in Case Packs

As a wholesaler, you sell to retailers in bulk, and retailers can only order in multiples, not as single units.

On Amazon, if you sold candle extenders you would sell them one at a time. The warehouse would pick a single unit, from a bin or box full of your products, and put that single unit into another box, label it, and ship it out the door. This is called pick-and-pack.

However, when you sell to retailers it's a simpler process and it starts at the factory.

Let's say that you sell your candle extenders in multiples of 8 at a time. To remind you, this means the retailer can order 8, or 16, or 24, or 32 units at a time, but never a single unit, or in any other amount that is not a multiple of eight.

This gives you a chance to make life easier on yourself.

Have the factory put the same number of units as your multiple, into the inner cartons. These would be called case-packs.

When a retailer places an order for a case-pack of eight candle extenders, the warehouse simply grabs an inner carton, slaps a label on it, and sends it out the door. Easy, quicker, and less expensive than single unit pick-and-pack.

PO (Purchase Order)

Large retailers will send you a purchase order (PO) which is a formal document that defines the quantity, delivery date, delivery location, price, payment terms, and other order information. Once you accept it, the PO becomes a legally binding contract.

After you deliver your products and they confirm that they have received them, you send an invoice in order to be paid. The big box retailer may pay in 30 days, 60 days, or more. It will be stipulated in the PO so it will not be a surprise.

Frankly this can feel like a long time. If you need payment sooner there are many options, including private financial companies that will pay you the amount you invoiced the next day, in exchange for a small interest fee that is due when the retailer pays the invoice. This is called factoring, also known as invoice financing, or accounts receivable financing.

Many financial companies offer this service, including invoice financing companies, factor companies, banks, fintech lenders, and credit unions.

Factoring has been a staple of the physical product business for many years. For small businesses and start ups it's the only way they can fulfill orders for big box stores.

✓ <u>Pro Tip:</u> A vessel travels from China to the west coast in approximately 16-24 days. Assume that it takes another 20 days to travel to the retailer's warehouse. That means a total of 36-44 days. Add another week turnaround in your 3PL, and you have a total of 43-51 days. Therefore, ask your factory for 60-day terms. This gives you enough time to ship products from China, get them to the retailer, and factor your invoice. All within time for you to pay your factory. Since its less than 60 days it's like getting a free loan to buy inventory.

This is why I advise my students and clients to negotiate payment terms at the same time they negotiate price.

Retail Sales Are Not Transactional

Each sale you make on Amazon is transactional. One and done. Sales made to retailers are long-term and ongoing. They will sell your products, reorder from you, and sell again. This repeats again and again and again from just a single sale. This leads to sustainable and predictable income, and frankly that leads to a better night's sleep.

TOP TWELVE TIPS
For Product Development and Sales

SUMMARY

I worked at Microsoft for 14 years. Many Microsoft alumni launch startups creating apps, games, and other amazing technology. Personally, I prefer physical products over digital products, but we are all entrepreneurs in our own way.

I know from my friends, and from hearing multiple pitches as part of an angel investment group, that software startups face a different financial reality than physical product developers.

Engineers and developers work tirelessly for months to put out a proof-of-concept, a beta, and eventually a finished product. They hope the entire time that they will eventually get financing from VCs or get bought by a private equity firm - earning millions, if not billions, of dollars.

They don't make a dime until they sell, so until that day they have to keep the doors open, lights on, and workers paid. The amount of money being spent each month can be quite large and is called the burn rate.

Physical products are different. We make money while we build and scale the company and eventually exit. Unlike apps and games, we focus on making sales and profits every month.

That puts us in control of our own destiny. We know from the day we launch whether we have a winning product or not. We don't have to wait years, burning money every month, until we can get feedback on a product that customers may not have wanted in the first place. We can physically see people's tasks become easier, watch children laughing with a new toy, or everyday problems get solved because of one innovative thinker.

The development itself is rewarding. There is nothing like the day the doorbell rings and a package is waiting with your product inside.

Colleagues who create digital products wonder why I prefer physical ones. I wonder the same thing about them. I'm convinced that once they try developing physical products they will never go back.

Of course there are no guarantees in our business. Everyone has hits and misses. There is always risk. But if you focus on WTP validation, confirm customer demand, keep your eye on the bottom line and always prioritize being profitable, then you have an incredible chance of having a successful product, making customers happy, and making a lot of money for yourself.

One further note. The WTP Product Development model that I talk about here and in my other books is new. I built this development model, with a constant emphasis on WTP, because it gives small business and entrepreneurs an advantage over large corporations. I believe the little guy deserves a chance to win.

I thank you for believing in the WTP product development path. I am humbled by the product successes of entrepreneurs who follow my WTP development process.

If you would like to learn more about the WTP process, manufacturing, designing products, negotiations, logistics, selling to retailers, Chinese factories, ensuring quality, the Canton Fair, or anything else to do with product development, please feel free to reach out to me. I would love to talk.

steven@productdevelopmentacademy.com

Thank you. Good Luck. Have fun. And make money.

ProductDevelopmentAcademy.com

CantonFairTrip.com

TOP TWELVE TIPS
For Product Development and Sales

www.ingramcontent.com/pod-product-compliance
Lightning Source LLC
Chambersburg PA
CBHW052338220526
45472CB00001B/475